**21st Century**
**Junior Library**

LOVED ONES WITH
DEPRESSION

Lacey Hilliard and
AnneMarie McClain

Loved Ones With

Published in the United States of America by Cherry Lake Publishing Group
Ann Arbor, Michigan
www.cherrylakepublishing.com

Reading Adviser: Beth Walker Gambro, MS, Ed., Reading Consultant, Yorkville, IL
Book Designer: Jen Wahi

Photo Credits: cover: © Ronnachai Palas/Shutterstock; page 5: © Monkey Business Images/Shutterstock; page 6–7: © Ground Picture/Shutterstock; page 8 (left): © BRO.vector/Shutterstock; page 8 (right): © fizkes/Shutterstock; page 9: © pixelheadphoto digitalskillet/Shutterstock; page 10: © myboys.me/Shutterstock; page 11 (top): © Mama Belle and the kids/Shutterstock; page 11 (bottom left): © islandboy_stocker/Shutterstock; page 11 (bottom right): © Monkey Business Images/Shutterstock; page 12: © fizkes/Shutterstock; page 13: © Prostock-studio/Shutterstock; page 14: © Halfpoint/Shutterstock; page 16: © fizkes/Shutterstock; page 17: © loreanto/Shutterstock; page 18 (left): © PeopleImages.com – Yuri A/Shutterstock; page 18 (right): ©KOTOIMAGES/Shutterstock; page 19: © alwie99d/Shutterstock; page 20–21: © fizkes/Shutterstock

Note from publisher: Websites change regularly, and their future contents are outside of our control. Supervise children when conducting any recommended online searches for extended learning opportunities.

Library of Congress Cataloging-in-Publication Data

Names: McClain, AnneMarie, author. | Hilliard, Lacey, author.
Title: Loved ones with depression / written by AnneMarie McClain and Lacey Hilliard.
Description: Ann Arbor, Michigan : Cherry Lake Publishing, [2023] | Series: Loved ones with | Audience: Grades 2-3 | Summary: "Loved Ones With Depression covers the basics of depression, what people with depression might experience, loving someone with depression, and showing love for others and yourself. Loved Ones With explores what it's like to watch loved ones go through unique and often difficult circumstances. Written in kid-friendly language, this social-emotional learning series supports readers' empathetic understanding of these experiences not only for their loved ones, but also for themselves. Guided exploration of topics in 21st Century Junior Library's signature style help readers to Look, Think, Ask Questions, Make Guesses, and Create"– Provided by publisher.
Identifiers: LCCN 2023004579 | ISBN 9781668927359 (hardcover) | ISBN 9781668928400 (paperback) | ISBN 9781668929872 (ebook) | ISBN 9781668931356 (pdf)
Subjects: LCSH: Depressed persons–Family relationships–Juvenile literature. | Children of depressed persons–Juvenile literature. | Depression, Mental–Juvenile literature.
Classification: LCC RC537 .M39265 2023 | DDC 618.92/8527–dc23/eng/20230310
LC record available at https://lccn.loc.gov/2023004579

Cherry Lake Publishing would like to acknowledge the work of the Partnership for 21st Century Learning, a network of Battelle for Kids. Please visit http://www.battelleforkids.org/networks/p21 for more information.

Printed in the United States of America
Corporate Graphics

# CONTENTS

# WHAT IS DEPRESSION?

Depression is a medical condition. It might happen when brain **chemicals** are at different levels than normal. Depression might happen because brains are different. It might happen because brains are injured.

Sometimes **genes** make depression more likely for a person. Depression may happen when dealing with other challenges. It may happen when dealing with other illnesses. It is never the depressed person's fault for having depression.

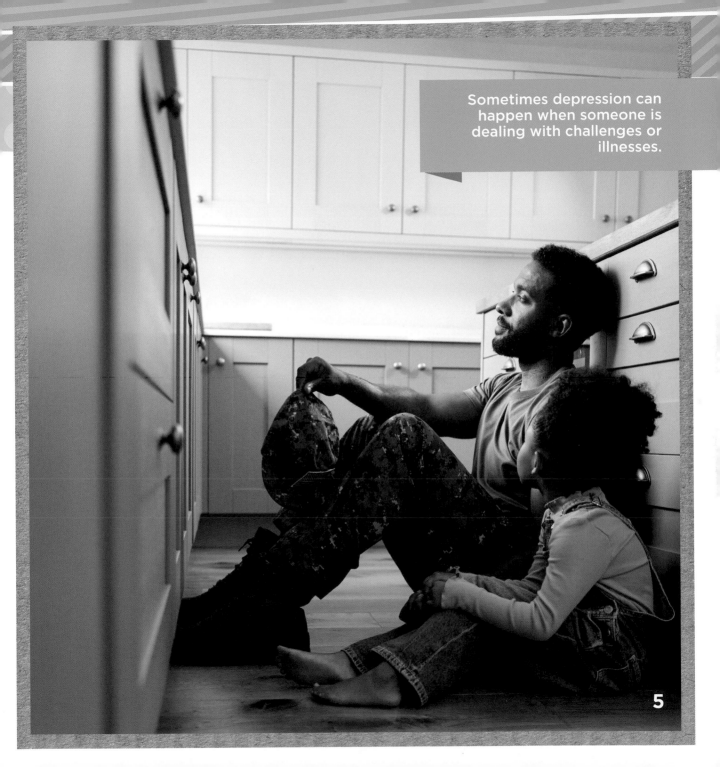

Sometimes depression can happen when someone is dealing with challenges or illnesses.

# WHAT PEOPLE WITH DEPRESSION MIGHT EXPERIENCE

Depression may look different in each person. You can't tell someone has depression by looking at them.

When someone is depressed, they may feel tired. They may have a hard time getting out of bed. They may have a hard time sleeping. They may not enjoy things they usually do. They may move slowly. They may eat more or less. They may have a

# Make a Guess!

Who in your community is supporting
people with depression?

hard time concentrating. They may feel guilt. They may want to be alone.

Sometimes people with depression may not feel like life is worth living for them. They might feel this way even if people love them. They might feel this way even if they seem happy.

Sometimes people hurt, or want to hurt, themselves. Some people die by suicide because of their depression. Sometimes these things can't be controlled.

Though you can't control how your loved one feels, you can be there for them when they are depressed.

When depression is treated, the symptoms might get better. Some people with depression take medicine. Some attend psychotherapy. Exercise and meditation may help. It can take time to figure out what might work best. Sometimes people don't get better. It's not fair how that works.

There are many ways to treat depression. In addition to talking with professional helpers, exercising, eating well, and being outside are a few of them.

It may be hard for someone to seek treatment. It may be hard to **recognize** they have depression. It may be hard to say they have depression. People may feel embarrassed. No one should make anyone feel bad for having depression.

Sometimes it's hard for people to realize they have depression.

People may need to go to the hospital for depression. They may need to go to a health care facility. Sometimes people go many times.

**Look!**

Here are people doing everyday things. You can't tell if any of them have depression. You can't know that just by looking at them.

Your loved one with depression is still the person you love.

14

# LOVING SOMEOME WITH DEPRESSION

If a loved one has depression, you might feel all kinds of emotions. You might not know how to feel. It is okay to feel however you feel.

It can be hard to see someone have depression. You might wish you could make the depression go away. Your loved one is still the person you love.

## Think!

How could you be a friend to someone with depression? How could you be a friend to someone whose loved one has depression?

People may worry that someone they love is depressed. People may worry they have depression. Talking with a health care expert may help. Experts can be **therapists** or doctors. Experts can try to help people and their families.

Grown-ups might need to focus their attention. They may need to focus on your loved one. You might have big feelings. You can ask for time with your grown-ups. People in the same family can need different things.

It's okay to ask for time with your grown-ups. People can need different things.

Professional helpers can work with people who have depression.

# SHOWING LOVE FOR OTHERS AND YOURSELF

There are ways you can show love for your loved one with depression. There are ways you can show love for yourself.

You can keep yourself feeling healthy and strong. It is important to take care of yourself, too.

You might want to let out your feelings by writing. You might want to try drawing. You might want to talk. You might want to talk to your loved one. You can let them know how much you love them. You might want to cry. You might want to snuggle with a pet. You might want to snuggle with someone you love. You can have fun and do the things you enjoy. You can still be you.

You might want to volunteer. You can volunteer with groups that support people with depression.

# Create!

Write a pretend letter to someone whose loved one has depression. What would you like them to know?

# Ask Questions!

## Things to know:

It is okay to talk about depression.

Many people get better. It is not always possible to get better.

Helpers want to stop depression and support people. Experts have learned about many things that can help. Helpers are working to make things better. Things can be better for people with depression.

Maybe you'll be one of the helpers one day. Maybe you already are.

21

# GLOSSARY

**chemicals** (KEH-mih-kuhlz) a group of atoms connected together that cause certain properties; the building blocks of everything in the universe

**emotions** (ih-MOH-shuhnz) feelings

**genes** (JEENZ) the code-like instructions in a body's cells

**psychotherapy** (sye-coh-THAIR-uh-pee) talking with someone or being with an animal to work through feelings or thoughts; also called therapy

**recognize** (REH-kuhg-nyez) to notice and understand what something is

**symptoms** (SIMP-tuhmz) the things that people feel or that can happen to them because of their illness

**therapists** (THAIR-uh-pists) people who work with someone during therapy

**treated** (TREE-tuhd) given medical attention or care

# LEARN MORE

## Books:

*A Kids Book About Depression* by Kileah McIlvain, A Kids Company About

*Pockets Full of Rocks* by Yair Engelberg, Magination Press and the American Psychological Association

*Ruby Finds a Worry* by Tom Percival, Bloomsbury Publishing

*Talking About Mental Health* by AnneMarie McClain & Lacey Hilliard, Cherry Lake Publishing

# INDEX

## ABOUT THE AUTHORS

**Lacey Hilliard** is a college professor, researcher, and parent. Her work is in understanding how grown-ups talk to children about the world around them. She particularly likes hearing what kids have to say about things.

**AnneMarie McClain** is an educator, researcher, and parent. Her work is about how kids and families can feel good about who they are. She especially loves finding ways to help kids and families feel seen in TV and books.